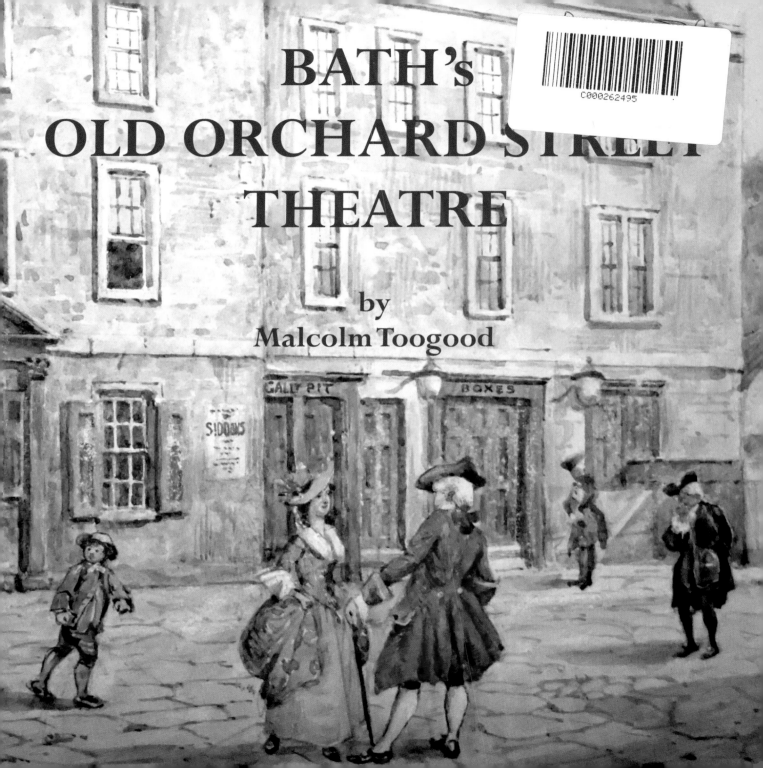

BATH's
OLD ORCHARD STREET
THEATRE

by

Malcolm Toogood

Cepenpark Publishing Ltd
10 Sandpiper Gardens
Chippenham
SN14 6YH

CepenPark Publishing Ltd

First Published in Great Britain in 2010 by Cepenpark Publishing Ltd

A catalogue record of this book
is available from the British Library
ISBN 978 0 9564230 0 9

Printed in Great Britain by
Butler Tanner & Dennis, Frome, Somerset

Contents

Acknowledgements

All books need more than just the author to form themselves from the ether, and there are many people to thank for their assistance in creating this one. Firstly, all at Old Orchard Street who have supported me in bringing the history together, in particular Trevor, Alan and Mike for delving into the deepest recesses of the historical records, and David for his unwavering encouragement. Also I must not forget Joan, who supplied some amazing Sarah Siddons memorabilia just at the right time.

Then there are all of the curators and librarians of the various Galleries, Museums, Libraries and Record Offices that helped find the evidence and images to support the text, specifically those in Bath at the Reference Library, Victoria Art Gallery and Bath in Time, without whom I would never have found the rare ones. Filling the historical image gaps, the band of photographers, Dan, Andy, Christina, Jess, Mark, and in particular Paul who was always available to take that one that I missed last time.

To my family and friends who have had to tolerate my head being buried (again) in the PC screen for weeks on end, in particular my long-suffering wife Kathy who still puts up with me after more than forty years of tangents. Thanks also to Terry, Jim and Andy for continuing to look interested on Thursday nights while I banged-on about another serendipity that had occurred that week.

But most of all, my thanks to you Ken for making this possible by introducing me to all of this history.

I hope you enjoy it

Malcolm Toovey

Foreword

As a Bathonian, I have been aware all of my life of the rich history of the City. This richness was enhanced through my father's recollections of some of its past glories, related as we rode through the streets together on his bus during my school holidays in the fifties, when everything seemed to be blackened shells and shades of grey imposed by the aftermath of the harsh years of war and rationing. As I grew into a teenager during the sixties, the City changed with the post war reconstruction, not much of it for the better, but as facades were cleaned and the rich creamy stone emerged from decades of soot-encrusted hibernation, parts of the City took on a cheerier persona.

I spent a lot of my business years working in the City, although the economics of a growing family dictated that we would live in the surrounding towns. However, I was still able to pass on my acquired knowledge to friends and clients that visited us, through trips to the various tourist attractions in and around the City. Interesting though the various tours were, few really engrossed my attention as much as those living descriptions from my father, someone who had lived within the largely unchanged streets of the years between the two world wars. Not, that is, until I retired and became involved with Old Orchard Street.

At first the building seemed to be just another old Georgian pile, kept up-together by its owners as best they could, whilst balancing the demands from the crumbling fabric against the limited depths of the pockets of their members. Not that they had done a bad job, far from it, considering that they have owned it for 140 years (and counting) and are still able to use it regularly with little drama.

It was when I began to learn its rich history that it took on a completely different character, that of a time machine that had stayed rooted to its terrestrial spot whilst the ethereal life of the City had flowed around and through it for over 250 years.

As I stood looking up at the stage, I could smell the smoke from the tallow candles as Sarah Siddons and William Keasberry tugged at the emotions of peers in their boxes and paupers in the upper gallery. I could visualise John Palmer having the inspiration to create a fleet of stage coaches that would enable his actors to travel quickly between his two theatres, not realising that a few years later they would change his life completely when put to a different use.

I could hear the fiery sermons of Bishop Baines delivered to a congregation of diverse denominations, all listening intently and as silent as the corpse of a member of the French nobility interred in the vaults below their feet.

I could feel the pride of John Stothert, standing upright and true as the Temple that he had helped to acquire for his Lodge was dedicated into use, giving them the permanent home they had desired for 140 years and that would remain as such for as long again into the future. And I could feel the shockwaves as the Luftwaffe blew the roof off, through a direct hit on the adjoining buildings, and sense the determination of my father's generation to not let them succeed in their tyranny.

There are many buildings that can evoke similar emotions throughout the City of Bath, but few that can do so under one roof through such close associations with so many of its leading citizens over so long a timespan. I hope that you will enjoy my brief window on this hidden gem.

Malcolm Toogood
August 2009

2

PART ONE

THEATRE
1750 to 1805

An Attraction for Bath

Bath has always been a magnet for pilgrimage. It has been a centre for worship from way back in pagan times, before the Romans arrived to usurp the local god of the spring as the deity for their Temple to Minerva. Later, in medieval times, it became the seat of an Augustine Abbey, founded by Offa, King of Mercia, in 781.

The benefits of taking the local spring waters, first discovered by Prince Bladud's errant pigs, were combined by the Romans with their later Temple to Sulis Minerva, to create one of the largest bathing complexes in Britannia. Later, Mineral Hospitals for healing the sick and the lame were created by the Abbey fathers. These were made more fashionable in the early 18th century by the self-appointed society 'Master of Ceremonies', Beau Nash, and later in that century purpose-built spa complexes were developed by architects Thomas Baldwin and John Wood the Younger. From these beneficial seasonal breaks, society events blossomed that incorporated entertainment and pastimes, out of which grew the tourist industry that now brings over a million visitors every year, flocking to the City from all over the world .

Above
Bladud in Exile
by Benjamin West
Royal Academy of Arts,
London.
Opposite
Map of Bath
c1694
by Gilmore
Bath Records Office

Although the Bath they visit still bears all of the hallmarks of those major historical attractions spreading back thousands of years through history, it is a vastly different, and larger, City than it was 300 years ago. At the turn of the century in 1700, Bath was still a small city whose wealth through the middle ages had been based on a wool industry that was, by then, in steep decline. The population of 2,000 were contained within a circular medieval wall that extended barely five-minutes' walk across. The North Gateway was at the top of the High Street where today's Guildhall stands, the

South Gate next to what is now Marks and Spencer. The West Gate was, unsurprisingly, at the bottom of Westgate Street, and the East Gate near the eastern end of the Abbey, where the Empire Hotel now overlooks the Recreation Ground.

There were few grand buildings within those walls and development beyond them was limited to tenements stretching a few hundred yards beyond the North Gate, along what are now Walcot and Broad Streets, and between the South Gate and the Avon Bridge, creating Southgate Street. The skyline was dominated by the Abbey building you see today, overlooking its own gardens enclosed by a wall breached by the Abbey Gate, at the bottom of what is now Abbey Green. From there, the Abbey Orchard stretched to the top of what is now the Southgate Shopping Centre, beyond which the land dropped down to the Ham, the meadows that stretched across to the crook in the River Avon at Widcombe.

Below
Richard 'Beau' Nash
by William Hoare
Bath in Time/Royal National Hospital for Rheumatic Diseases, Bath

It was not until the mid-1720s that, under Richard Nash's influence and prompted by the regular arrival of the great and the good visiting the city, the need to entertain these visitors encouraged the building of grand halls and ballrooms. At the turn of the century the city had a theatre, of sorts, located in Upper Borough Walls on the site later occupied by the Mineral Water Hospital. Contemporary accounts, however, suggest that the building was little more than an adapted stable, a situation that caused huge embarrassment to the local burghers in 1702 during the State Visit to the city by Queen Anne. Her entourage included the entire Drury Lane Theatre Company, who found themselves only able to provide within that building *'an entertainment of sorts for Her Majesty'* during her stay.

A subsequent subscription among *'people of the highest rank'* raised thirteen hundred pounds to demolish the existing building and replace it with a purpose-built theatre, but it would appear that attending a play in this building was a particularly uncomfortable experience for theatre-goers. As a consequence, it only attracted

The Palmers at Orchard Street

There have been numerous accounts written in the 20th Century relating the period of Bath history between 1750 and 1785, some of which present John Palmer as a multi-facetted personality with various business interests. In these, he is any manner of combinations of a brewer, tallow-chandler, post office comptroller, architect, Member of Parliament, theatre-proprietor, Mayor of Bath and even an actor. These confusions are easier to unravel when it is understood that there was not just one John Palmer involved with Orchard Street during that period, but four.

In 1764, the John Palmer who founded the theatre handed-over the management of the company to his son, also called John. Bath had become the main focal point for social activity outside of the capital and consequently, throughout the winter months, it was thronging with visitors of noble rank. In order to capitalise on this, John Palmer Junior set about raising both the profile and standing of his theatre. The interior was remodelled and, when re-opened to the public in March 1767, the results included an elevated dome incorporating Apollo and the Muses in relief, described as *'esteemed, in fancy, elegance, and construction, inferior to none in Europe'*

Above
John Palmer
by an unknown artist
Private Collection
Right
John Palmer Jr
by Thomas Beach
Victoria Art Gallery, B&NES Council

In 1768, John Palmer Junior presented a petition in London for a Royal Warrant for the Theatre, which was granted by special Act of Parliament. This enabled him to change the name of the establishment to the Theatre Royal, a privilege only enjoyed at that time by the two leading London theatres in Drury Lane and Covent Garden, making it the first provincial theatre to be given that honour.

This status upgrade, enabled him to attract top theatre companies, along with some of the leading stars in the English theatre. In 1771, he appointed the well-known Bath actor William Keasberry as the theatre's actor-manager. This proved to be an excellent move, as not only was Keasberry well-respected throughout the profession, he was also, somewhat unusually for a thespian of that era, an efficient business manager as well.

John Palmer Junior also had a keen eye for talent. During his early years in charge, he undertook regular talent-scouting trips around other provincial theatres, where he recruited up-and-coming actors for the company at Bath. It was clearly this activity that set the foundations for the theatre's high-reputation as a nursery for developing such talent in the latter part of the century. The first major actor to emerge through Orchard Street made his first appearance there in 1772 under the 'nom de theatre' of Mr Courtney. 'Courtney' was somewhat unsure not only of his own abilities, but also of whether he wanted to pursue a career on the stage at all, hence his initial reluctance to use his real name. However, the audience was not so reticent and the response to his debut performance was instant, the Bath Chronicle reporting the following day that:

"Last night a young gentleman, whose name is Courtney, made his first appearance on our stage in the character of Hamlet, which he supported throughout with so much ease, judgment and propriety in action as well as expression, as gained him the warmest plaudits of the whole audience. And we cannot help congratulating the admirers of the tragic muse on so valuable an acquisition to our Theatre."

Above
Mr Keasberry of Bath by Ralph Stennet
Victoria Art Gallery, B&NES Council
Left
John Henderson by Thomas Gainsborough,
National Portrait Gallery, London

A few days later, he returned as Richard III, to similar acclaim and continued for the next two months covering all of the main tragic roles. By that time he had concluded that it would be an actor's life for him, and during December he appeared in Henry IV as Hotspur, under his real name of John Henderson. Henderson appeared as part of the company at Orchard Street for five seasons before the inevitable call to the London stage, which came at the end of the 1777/8 season. Before his career was cut tragically short by a fever just eight years later, Henderson achieved a reputation for tragic acting that came close to the great David Garrick, whose mantle he assumed after the latter's death in 1779. Theatre-goers in Bath were doubtful that Orchard Street could survive such a major loss, but their fears would be short-lived, as Palmer had already secured the services for the following season of a then-unknown actress called Sarah Siddons.

In 1774, the building was again redesigned. The architect for this work was another John Palmer, who would also be involved with the design of the building that would replace Orchard Street thirty years later. Because of the theatre links, this John Palmer is often confused with the owner of Orchard Street, as they were contemporaries in the city. However, they were not the same person. In fact they were not even related, either to each other or to yet another John Palmer, the London actor, who occasionally appeared in productions at Orchard Street, and was particularly noted for his portrayal of Joseph Surface in Sheridan's *'School for Scandal'*.

Below
John Palmer the Architect
English School
Victoria Art Gallery, B&NES Council
Right
John Palmer the Actor by an unknown artist
National Portrait Gallery, London

With the work completed, and released from the day-to-day management of Orchard Street, John Palmer Junior turned his attentions on creating a mirror-image of it in nearby Bristol. He acquired the lease for a theatre in King Street and, in 1778, he also obtained a Royal Warrant for that establishment, meaning that he could offer touring companies the opportunity of staging back-to-back performances in two high-status theatres within fifteen miles of each other.

As part of the logistics for staging the same production in both of his theatres, Palmer set-up a coach service between the two establishments, to enable the efficient transport back and forth of stagehands, props and, most importantly, actors. This innovation would eventually lead John Palmer Junior to a career change that would take him away from the theatre and into public life.

John Palmer Junior also used the coaches to make trips to the capital to visit theatre company owners. He realised that he could physically make the journey to the capital in less than a day, whereas it took the mail three days to make the same trip. This was because the existing mail service involved the use of a number of relay riders passing the mailbags from one to the other. He suggested to the Post Office that a coach service could be utilised far more efficiently and, although he initially met with stout resistance, he eventually persuaded the Chancellor of the Exchequer, William Pitt, to permit him to run a trial, which Palmer would fund himself.

The trial was conducted in 1784 and Palmer's coach completed the run from Bristol to London in just sixteen hours, less than half the time it took the competing relay of riders. Pitt was so impressed that he immediately authorised the establishment of the Bristol to London Mail Coach service, plus four additional routes. By the end of the following year, the number of services had trebled and, in 1786, John Palmer Junior was made Surveyor and Comptroller General of the Post Office.

His zeal for reform within the Post Office brought him into constant conflict with the establishment within the organisation, resulting in his eventual dismissal in 1792. He subsequently entered politics and went on to become Mayor of Bath in 1796, then MP for the City in 1801. After standing-down from Parliament in favour of his son, Charles, he was again made Mayor of Bath in 1809. He received many honours for his revolutionary work with the Postal service, including the freedom of a number of cities associated with the Mail Coach service. More information on John Palmer and his mail coaches can be found in the Bath Postal Museum.

When Palmer was appointed to the Post Office, he sold the Theatre Royal Company to his manager William Keasberry and another actor, William Dimond. Keasberry continued as manager until 1795, during which time the theatre played to capacity houses throughout each season. Probably because it was managed by actors, the theatre company continued to encourage new talent, many actors graduating from it to become household names at both Covent Garden and Drury Lane. These latter years of the 18th century were also marked by the rise of local playwrights, such as Richard Sheridan, whose plays were regularly performed at Orchard Street, adding more caché to the establishment.

Below
William Dimond
as Hamlet
by Thomas Barker
Victoria Art Gallery,
B&NES Council

After Keasberry retired, Dimond took over the management and the success of the enterprise continued, to the point that it was outgrowing the building, which due to the nearby developments now planned to be erected on the Ham, could not be enlarged. This was not the case in the sister Theatre in Bristol, so it became obvious that the Bath theatre required a new home. As the new developments springing-up to the north and west had effectively moved the main focal point of the city, the new site was selected in Beauford Square.

The new building was designed by the architect John Palmer, mentioned previously, who had succeeded Thomas Baldwin to the post of City Architect for Bath in 1792. As well as the New

Theatre Royal, he was also responsible for a number of notable Bath landmarks, including St James' Square, Lansdown Crescent, New Bond Street and St James' Church, which stood on the corner of Orchard Street and Stall Street until it was demolished in the 1950s, having been devastatingly-bombed in the second world war. His New Theatre Royal opened its doors for the first time in 1805 with a capacity of more than three times that of its predecessor. It remains as the City's main theatre to this day.

After 55 years filled with the sounds of laughter and tragedy, the original Theatre Royal in Orchard Street fell silent and empty.

Bath Theatre Royal

Georgian theatres had a very different atmosphere to those we experience today. There was little of the reverence that modern audiences award their performers, at least when the performances are good, which in today's professional companies they invariably are.

When we view a play in the 21st Century, once the curtain rises, the auditorium is unlit and modern lighting design focuses our attention firmly on the stage itself. Not so in the days of Orchard Street, where the auditorium and stage were all lit to even levels, albeit by tallow candles, but still ensuring that everybody could see everybody else in equal light. This arrangement was not without its perils and, in the early days of Orchard Street, there were constant complaints from patrons regarding the damage sustained to their expensive attire by the hot drips from the illuminations.

The constant flux and movement in the audience was very obvious, again not dissimilar to that experienced at a modern-day rock concert, where some members of the audience seem almost incapable of lasting more than two songs without the benefit of replenishment. Consequently, it was not just the actors that would make dramatic entrances, or exits. The more flamboyant the theatre-goer, the more likely they would make an impressive entrance to their chosen place in the auditorium. Furthermore, whereas today it is almost unheard of for a member of the audience to leave during a performance, in the 18th century it would not be unusual for a patron to leave once their favourite actor had completed their role, even if that were some time before the curtain fell.

Opposite Exterior of Bath's Theatre Royal in Orchard Street by T Woodfall *Bath in Time / Bath Central Library Collection* This print shows that the exterior is little changed 200 years later. Note the steps in the lower right corner that led down to the carriage forecourt. The building just visible stepped-back to the left is No. 5 Pierrepont Place

Actors would greet these interruptions with a reaction tailored to their mood, sometimes welcoming their new 'guests' reverently, if they happened to be a personal patron, but more often mocking in a manner not dissimilar to that experienced today from our stand-up comedians. The bawdiness of the atmosphere continued

throughout the performance and the interaction between audience and cast could often be more entertaining than the actual play being performed.

The histrionics of the actors on stage were also quite different. A lot of plays were written in such a way that, once the actor's part had made its entrance, it then remained on stage, albeit in the background, until the scene ended. In these circumstances, it was not unusual for a 'star' to upstage their fellow actors by exhibiting total boredom with the performance of every other part, whilst awaiting their next 'big moment'.

All of this was further enhanced by the layout of the theatre. In 1750, when Orchard Street opened, the auditorium was the size of the main hall as you see it today. The layout, however, differed considerably. In front of the stage was the pit, where it was standing room only and the entrance price was cheaper. At the stage end the floor level was lower, almost to the level of the vault floor. From there it sloped upwards to the back of the auditorium, where the entrance doors opened onto the street.

There were no advance tickets for the standing areas so, as the evening's performance would commence at 6 o'clock, early playbills often included a note that *"Ladies and Gentlemen are desired to send their servants to keep places by half an hour after four o'clock"*. This practice often resulted in disruption, due to the performance commencing whilst the footmen of late arrivals were still holding their employers' places and, having become bored with standing around, they would show little interest in the play, instead bantering loudly with other similarly-mooded servants across the crowd.

Along each side of the auditorium were three additional levels, the lower containing boxes and the upper two galleries, the uppermost just under the ceiling. For some performances, the more favoured or affluent patrons would have been given seats at the side of the stage, which led to some very interesting situations. On one infamous occasion, a patron seated on one side of the stage became so bored with the performance, that he got up and crossed the stage to talk with a friend seated on the other side – whilst the performance was in progress. This led to an altercation with one of the actors and swords were drawn!

The first remodelling of the interior in 1767 added the decorous dome, among other things, but did little for the comforts of the audience. The acoustics after the dome had been added were described as 'dreadful' and ventilation was virtually non-existent, meaning that the heat created by a full house was a constant cause for complaint by theatregoers. So, in 1774, the interior of the building was again redesigned and the auditorium enlarged by adding a further 25 feet to the rear of the building, providing an entrance lobby and crush room at ground floor level. Above it

**Right
Interior of the
Theatre in
Orchard Street**
by Nixon
*Victiria Art Gallery,
B&NES Council*

seven grand boxes, each named after a King, were added in a fan shape. Each box contained five rows of benches, each row with five seats, and it was somewhat fitting that the central box, effectively the best seats in the house, was named after King Bladud, the founder of the City.

This allowed the stage to also be remodelled to a classical style based upon a blend of a Greek Proscenium and a Roman Scenae Frons, incorporating the four pairs of Doric and Ionic columns that you see today, as well as creating a musicians area at the front of the pit, thus

moving the audience back some six feet from the stage. Stage boxes were added at the sides, removing the need for stage seats. Just one of these boxes remains to the left of the stage, providing an indication of how they would have looked at that time.

More importantly, the dome, together with the adornments so gloriously praised just a few years earlier, was removed, allowing the roof to be remodelled, incorporating a displacement ventilation system supplying fresh air equally diffused across the auditorium, which is still in working use today. Finally, rows of benches were added to the pit and altogether this provided for a much more comfortable evening's entertainment. Prices were three shillings for a box seat, two shillings for the pit, then one shilling and sixpence for the middle galleries and one shilling for the upper. The building remained in this configuration for the rest of its life as a theatre, the only other major change being externally.

In 1781, Palmer persuaded the City Council to build a new coach road linking St James' Street to Orchard Street, which enabled his stage-coaches to reach a large forecourt and stabling he had created at the side of the theatre. As well as enabling loading and unloading directly into the building's storage areas, this arrangement also provided parking accommodation for around fifty carriages during evening performances. Orchard Street was, by then, becoming beyond reasonable walking distance for the majority of its more well-heeled patrons staying in the fashionable new accommodation to the north and west of the city. From reports of the time, there was a measure of support for moving the Theatre itself to a new building in that area, a move that would ultimately be inevitable. However, due probably to this astute change by Palmer, the relocation would not happen until nearly 25 years later, because theatre-goers were not only provided with the convenience of being able to ride by carriage to the theatre, but also the ability to 'arrive' when so doing.

Right
Map of Bath
c1795 by C Harcourt Masters
Bath Records Office
This detail shows the new coach road leading to the forecourt for the Theatre (L) and associated stabling. The dotted line shows the position of the medieval City Wall

The coach road is shown on maps of the time as an extension of Orchard Street, but in fact it was at the level of the Ham, which was at the basement level of the building. The public entrances in Orchard Street were, therefore, a floor-level higher, so a flight of steps was constructed from the courtyard to the theatre entrance, for use by theatre-goers arriving by carriage. It was around this time that the higher level was renamed to Old Orchard Street to distinguish it from the coachway, which was named New Orchard Street. They were finally linked at the same level when the houses in Henry Street were constructed in the early 19th century, the eastern end of New Orchard Street being raised to make the continuous thoroughfare into Henry Street as it is to this day.

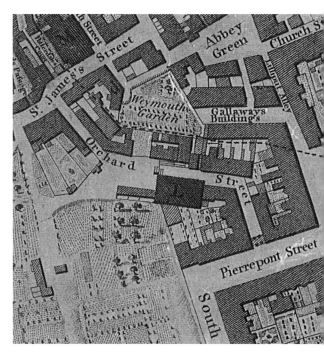

To aid with financing this addition, Palmer increased ticket prices, but this was an unpopular move that was subsequently reversed by Keasberry and Dimond when they took over the management in 1786, a move that rewarded them with full houses for their entire first season.   Even so, a full house would only return in the order of £75 per night, which meant that company actors' salaries had to be kept under strict control. These 'basic' salaries were enhanced through a subscription book kept in the box office, where *those ladies and gentlemen could subscribe who should wish to pay a complement to the merits of any performers.* This explains why benefit performances, where the management waived their ticket receipts entirely, would often raise more than double the normal full house take for the beneficiary, a one-off 'bonus' from one performance that could effectively double their entire annual salary.

This aspect was clearly not lost on the actors, both old and new, which may explain why so many of the graduates to the London stage were happy to return later in their careers for short seasons and benefits. Besides the obvious stars like Siddons, Kemble and Henderson, the list of actors in the Orchard Street company between 1775 and 1805 reads like a roll-call of the best actors on the English stage at the time, with names like Mr Blanchard, Mr Murray, Mr & Mrs Bernard, Mr Incledon, Miss Wallis and Mr Elliston regularly appearing in major roles on Covent Garden and Drury Lane playbills within ten years of first appearing in minor ones at Orchard Street.

Clearly, what was created in what is now a tiny provincial back street, through the initial entrepreneurial vision of the Palmers and the subsequent management of the experienced actors Keasberry and Dimond, has a truly unique place in theatrical history that has remained largely uncelebrated for 200 years.

PART TWO

CHAPEL
1809 to 1863

Left
Bath Abbey
from the
North-East
by JMW Turner
Tate Gallery, London
This painting from
1791 shows how
closely developers
were allowed to
build next to the
Abbey back then.
It also shows the
Duke of Chandos'
mansion in Orange
Grove, which is
now an open space,
as can be seen in
the inset photo of
the same view
today.
Photo Bath in Time /
Bath Preservation Trust

The Benedictines of Bath

There has been a major church in Bath since the 7th Century, when Osric, King of Hwicce granted the Abbess Berta one hundred hides of land for the establishment of a convent in the southernmost town of his kingdom. It was later converted to a monastery by the Bishop of Worcester, which by the end of the following century was known as *"that most famous monastery at Bath."*

A hundred years after its foundation, King Offa of Mercia took the monastery from the Bishop and rebuilt the church on the site of the original pagan temple in the town. It was obviously an impressive building for its time, as even two hundred years later it was being described as *'marvellously built'*. Its prestige was elevated further when King Edgar was crowned the first King of the English there in 973. Edgar had encouraged the monks to adopt the order of St Benedict and hence the establishment of a Benedictine Abbey was made, under Abbot Aelfheah, who would later rise to the highest church post in the land as Archbishop of Canterbury, where he was martyred in 1012 and subsequently canonised as St Alphege.

Above Right Osric King of Hwicce Statue in Gloucester Cathedral Close *Photo by kind permission of Nash Ford Publishing*

After the Norman invasion, William II's personal physician, John de Villula, was granted the City and became Bishop of Wells and Abbot of Bath. The monastery was already extremely wealthy, so de Villula moved his Episcopal seat from Wells to Bath, before setting to work on a larger cathedral building, which would be dedicated to St Peter & St Paul. He died before the building was half-built and, despite a serious fire, it was eventually completed in 1156. Joint cathedral status was subsequently awarded by Pope Innocent and the first Bishop of Bath & Wells, Roger of Salisbury, was appointed in 1245. Later bishops, however, favoured Wells, so Bath Cathedral became run-down, eventually falling mainly into ruins.

When Bishop Oliver King surveyed what was left of the Cathedral in 1500, he ordered the Prior to dedicate himself to rebuilding it, but on a smaller scale. The Abbey building that you see today is effectively the results of that instruction. It is less than half the size of the Norman Cathedral, the floorplan of which spread all the way out to the east wall of the city, overlooking what is now the Parade Gardens. The work was completed just in time for the last incumbent, Prior Holloway, to surrender it to the crown in the form of King Henry VIII, who dissolved it, stripping everything valuable and leaving the shell to decay. His daughter Elizabeth I, however, decided it should be restored again as the Anglican parish church for the City and this work was completed in about 1620.

**Below
The Norman Cathedral c1400**
Model displayed in the Bath Abbey Vaults. Note how close it was to the City Walls compared to today's Abbey
*By kind permission of the Bath Abbey Heritage Vaults Museum
Photo Paul Mallon*

After the establishment of the Church of England, those deemed guilty of nonconformity were termed recusants and were subject to civil penalties which were, essentially, taxes imposed on those not observing the new religion. Failure to pay these 'taxes' would result in forfeitures and sometimes, especially in the earlier part of that period, harsher criminal penalties. Catholics formed a large proportion of recusants and were those to whom the term was initially applied.

During the Stuart period, the level to which these laws were enforced varied region by region and it would appear that Bath was one of the more lenient cities, presumably a local recognition that it would not retain the numbers of visitors it received to partake of the waters unless it was, quietly, somewhat liberal in its attitudes towards its guests. That relaxed atmosphere allowed a clandestine Benedictine Mission to remain in Bath, although no longer attached to the Abbey itself. There were certainly a number of prominent recusant families that continued to reside, quite undisturbed, in and around the city. One of these, the Carne family, owned the land and buildings in Upper Borough Walls where the city's first theatre, mentioned earlier, had been located.

The new chapel opened in December 1809 with a seating capacity of upwards of one thousand. To illustrate the importance of this chapel to the national mission, at the consecration service the 'Agnus Dei' was sung by Angelica Catalani, the finest Italian soprano of her age, who was living and working in England at the time, having left her previous home in France in 1806 in protest at Napoleon's rule. In 1812, some of the old dressing rooms in the upper part of the building were utilised for a girl's school, then in 1815 more were opened -up for a boy's school. The schools were administered by separate committees, who rented the rooms from the chapel along with rooms for the schoolmaster and schoolmistress in the next-door property, No. 5 Pierrepont Place, a building that had also been purchased by the Mission.

In 1817, a new principle missioner arrived from the Monastery at Ampleforth in Yorkshire to take over the running of the chapel. Peter Augustine Baines was an ambitious Lancastrian, who brooked no fools and had a self -driven destiny to fulfil. An early report to the Bath Mission from him indicated that the properties it owned were in a poor state:

"I found it necessary to incur great expenses not only in the chapel, but in all the houses and tenements belonging to it, which had been neglected, and some of which were in a state of complete dilapidation. The house next door was let to the school committee and underlet by the tenant to a number of beggars in separate apartments for half a crown a week. The rooms adjoining and over the chapel were tenanted in the same manner."

Above
Angelica Catalani
by Elisabeth Louise
Vigee Le Brun
Sotheby's Picture Library

He quickly set about bringing all of the properties in his care into a better state of order. Long leases were arranged on the Corn Street Chapel and the old presbytery in St James Parade, then with some of the proceeds a house was rented for the new presbytery just around the corner at No. 2 Pierrepont Place. Some years later, this property was also purchased by the Mission. No. 5 Pierrepont Place was improved and a Mrs Hippisley was appointed to run the lodgings, where the schoolmaster and schoolmistress continued to be accommodated along with the organist and 'the woman who takes care of the chapel'. Mrs Hippisley also ran a repository on the ground floor of number five for the sale of devotional articles, the 1826 edition of the "Bath Directory" recording a bookshop there where *"a general assortment of Catholic Books, etc, may be had."*

To finance improvements to the chapel, an appeal was launched in 1818 for donations. This met with some opposition, including from the lay-trustees that managed the finances, but by July that year this had clearly been overcome because a builder had been contracted to carry-out the changes, at a cost of eight hundred pounds. This is the point at which the windows were inserted high in the eastern wall to allow natural light into the interior. The improvements and additions were clearly effective, as in 1825 the "Original Bath Guide" reported that *"of late years, considerable additions and ornamental improvements have taken place in the chapel, which already contained an excellent organ and a brilliant choir."*

Baines was a popular and well-known preacher. Cardinal Wiseman said of him at the time that he was *"considered by all that heard him one of the most eloquent and earnest preachers they had ever attended"*. He preached regularly at the Orchard Street Chapel, his somewhat controversial sermons attracting a great deal of attention including that of the Anglican Archdeacon of Bath, Dr Charles Moysey. The two exchanged a series of letters during the 1820's which were later collectively published as the *'Baines Defence'*.

In 1823, Baines was appointed as coadjutor to Bishop Collingridge, who he succeeded as Vicar Apostolic of the Western District in 1829, immediately setting forth on what would be his legacy, the founding of Prior Park College. By then, Orchard Street Chapel was under the joint care of Dr Thomas Brindle, a close friend of Baines since his Ampleforth days, and Father Ralph Cooper, the latter taking sole charge when Dr Brindle moved to Prior Park to assist Bishop Baines with establishing the college there. Father Cooper remained in charge until 1846, making him by far the longest incumbent of Orchard Street Chapel. However, almost immediately on taking sole charge he found himself at the centre of political wranglings that were none of his making.

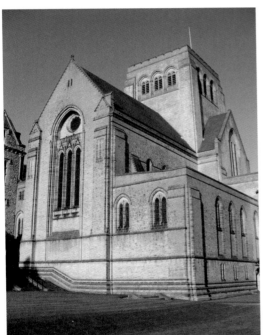

As was customary at that time, chapels covered their running costs by charging annual subscriptions for the pew seats. The chapel was part of the Benedictine Mission and therefore their financial responsibility; the Vicar Apostolic was a direct appointment of Rome and funded separately. Bishop Baines, being a Benedictine appointee, appears to have somewhat blurred the demarcation lines, because in 1830 he instructed Father Cooper to submit the seat rents to the Vicariate. The situation escalated to a high level very quickly. On November 20th 1830 the president of the English Benedictine Congregation, John Birdsall, instructed Father Cooper to issue a printed leaflet to the congregation as they entered the chapel for High Mass that day. The leaflet read:

"To the Congregation of the Catholic Chapel in Orchard Street, Bath: As the season is now at hand when Subscribers to this chapel usually renew their subscriptions for their sittings, the said subscribers are hereby requested by the owners of the chapel, that on account of certain hindrances now put in the way of those subscriptions being received by the rightful incumbents, they will withhold their subscriptions for a time, until the question arising out of the new order of things attempted to be introduced be decided. In the meantime Subscribers will continue to be admitted on producing their present tickets till further notice be given. J Birdsall"

**Above
Ampleforth
Abbey**
Photo Jo Jakeman

Bishop Baines and Dr Brindle were unaware of the handbill until they entered the building to conduct the service. Baines, who was not a stranger to controversy, immediately summoned Father Cooper and, under threat of suspension, ordered him to collect the subscriptions and submit them to the Vicariate. However, this was one cause that Baines was not destined to win. Once Birdsall, who it appears was a long-standing adversary, reminded Baines of the source of his original appointment, the matter was resolved in favour of the Chapel. Poor Father Cooper, having suffered such a stressful experience, appears to have been able to settle to a reasonably tranquil incumbency thereafter.

Bishop Baines, however, was not quite finished with the matter, subsequently withdrawing both himself and his assistant Dr Brindle from the Orchard Street Chapel to set up a rival establishment on the northern slopes of the City in Portland Place. Mission-wise, this was probably a desirable move, as the Catholic population had grown sufficiently in that area to justify it. However, the actual motives were questionable, and the Bishop received direct censure from the Pope for setting-up *'altar against altar'*. The Portland Place chapel was not a great success and was closed down a few years later, after which Baines appears to have reconciled his differences with Orchard Street, where he continued to preach occasionally until his untimely death in 1843.

In 1850, the Western District became the Diocese of Clifton and, in the same year, John Clement Worsley took charge of the Orchard Street Chapel. He had originally arrived eight years earlier, and served as assistant to both Father Cooper and his successor Jerome Jenkins. Worsley was clearly a forward-thinker, and he took charge at a time when the building of purpose-designed churches within the Catholic community was gathering pace.

His first priority, however, was the need for a new school building, as the demand for places had outgrown the accommodation in the chapel itself. The new school was erected directly across the road from the chapel and opened in 1852, and is the Manvers Hall building that is still there today. Both Boys and Girls schools were

provided, plus an Infants School catering for children 'from the age of two years'. By 1853, the infants' school alone had more than fifty pupils, perhaps unsurprisingly as it was the only school of its type in the City at that time.

Father Worsley's next move was to organise a dedicated site for Catholic burials in the city, to replace the unhealthy scenario that he had inherited beneath the Chapel, where the vaults had amassed some 300 tombs. In 1856, he purchased a parcel of land from the Prior Park Estate which became Perrymead Cemetery. A small chapel was erected there in 1859 and the transference of bodies from Orchard Street was completed in 1863, although a number of memorial tablets were left behind, some of which are on display in the Museum.

His final major task at Orchard Street commenced in 1861, when he organised the purchase of land from the Manvers Estate on the banks of the Avon opposite South Parade that had been part of the old Bath Priory orchard. On 6th October 1863, the new church of St John the Evangelist was consecrated and the congregation at Orchard Street transferred there along with Father Worsley, who continued in charge of St John's until his death in 1885.

After just over 325 years, the Benedictine Mission to Bath had travelled a full circle of history, but physically just a few hundred yards. It once again inhabited a place of worship on ground that it had originally owned nearly a thousand years earlier.

As a result, and after another 55 years of use, the Old Orchard Street building again echoed only to the sound of silence.

PART THREE

MASONIC HALL

1865 to date

December 28 1732.

The Lodge met at Brother Robinson's, the Bear, in Bath, and regularly form'd themselves.

Present.

Mr Hugh Kennedy   Master.

Mr Wm Howell   }
Mr Stoph: Martin   } Wardens.

Members.

Mr George Rainsford.
Mr Charles Gomm.
Mr Thos Collins.
Mr Johnson Robinson.
Mr St John Smyth.
Mr Joseph Wooby.
Mr Christopher Fleming.

Left
Minute Book of the Bear Inn Lodge showing the first page for their meeting on 28th December 1732
Bath Masonic Hall Trust

Right
Elias Ashmole by John Riley
National Portrait Gallery, London

Previous Page
Bath Masonic Hall as it is today
Photo Dan Brown

Temples of Stone

The origins of Freemasonry derive from various craft and trade guilds that evolved during medieval times, specifically those associated with stonemasons constructing the great cathedrals and castles of the time. By the mid-17th century, some of these had evolved into a gentlemen's society. One of the earliest published mentions of the organisation was in the diary of Elias Ashmole, founder of the Ashmolean Museum in Oxford, who mentioned his first visit to a Lodge at his father-in-law's house in 1646.

Early records are sparse, mainly due to the uncertain political climate during the 1688 Revolution when many private Lodges destroyed their hand-written records for fear, among other things, of making unfortunate disclosures. The Grand Master in the latter years of the 17th century is reputed to have been Sir Christopher Wren, but whether due to his prolific architectural activities, or merely to his pre-occupation with completing St Paul's Cathedral, meetings were held irregularly.

The various Lodges that existed at that time remained primarily independent until, on 24th June 1717, four London Lodges came together at the Goose and Gridiron public house near St Paul's Cathedral to create what would be the first Grand Lodge in the world. In 1723, The Grand Lodge of England, as it was named, published *'The Constitutions of Masonry'*, essentially the organisation's first uniform rulebook, and from this action additional Lodges in England, and Grand Lodges throughout the world, began to be deputised and subsequently warranted. From those beginnings, the organisation has grown to encompass over 8,000 Lodges serving over 300,000 members in the UK today, plus many more worldwide.

The first Deputised Lodge to be formed outside of London had its inaugural meeting in 1724 at the Queen's Head in Cheap Street, Bath, under the guidance of the then Deputy Grand Master of the order, Dr John Desaguliers, the philosopher, engineer and former assistant to Sir Isaac Newton. Among the founding members of the lodge were the Dukes of Bedford and St Albans, the Earl of Lichfield, Viscount Cobham, who was installed as Master of the Lodge, and Richard Nash.

The earliest surviving minutes for a Bath Lodge are of a meeting held at the Bear Inn on December 28th 1732, and it will be noted that these indicate that it *"met at Brother Robinson's, the Bear in Bath."* The new landlord of the Bear Inn at that time was a Mr Robinson and the name of Mr Johnson Robinson appears in the list of members. He also appears on the Masters Roll of Royal Cumberland Lodge in the Ante-Room at Orchard Street as being in the Master's Chair in 1736.

The Bear Inn was also in Cheap Street, next door to the Queen's Head on the opposite side of the entrance to Cock Lane, now Union Passage. It was the largest inn in the city at that time, occupying most of the area that is now the pedestrianised part of Union Street, indicating that membership had expanded beyond what could be accommodated in the smaller public house. By 1768, the Bear Inn Lodge had moved to the White Hart Inn, just fifty yards away down Stall Street, opposite the entrance to the Abbey Churchyard.

A Lodge meeting could take around two hours to complete, dependent on the amount and type of business to be conducted. After the formal activities of the evening were completed, most lodge members would then repair to a local hostelry for dinner together. It is therefore easy to understand the appeal of using rooms in public houses for meetings so that the dinner afterwards could be conducted in the same room, allowing the proceedings to run through uninterrupted. One of the other reasons was that it would appear that it was not unusual to partake of certain substances no longer allowed during Lodge meetings. In his short history of Royal Cumberland Lodge written in 1873, Thomas Ashley relates of the times of the Bear Inn Lodge:

"It would be strange in these times to see charges for wine and tobacco in our minutes, though we might not object to the good old days when wine was two shillings a bottle. But these were always supplied in the Lodge Room to our Ancient Brethren, it taking several bottles to audit the Treasurer's Account, and when that was done, and the balance struck and carried out, a postscript added of 'one bottle more' and that deducted from the balance. The zeal with which this was pursued occasioned complaints of the late hours they kept, as well as running-up a long bill for candles, the consideration of which they postponed from time to time, and eventually with much difficulty discharged."

Below
The White Hart
Inn by J C Maggs
Bath Masonic Hall Trust

In the early 1750s, a group of freemasons in London took issue with Grand Lodge and formed a rival Antients Grand Lodge utilising their own version of the constitutions that they claimed was based upon more ancient principles. They referred to Premier Grand Lodge as 'The Moderns'. This schism in the organisation could have caused major problems, but these never arose and the two co-existed, essentially because each ignored the existence of the other. All pre-existing Lodges remained part of Premier Grand Lodge, hence the Bear Inn Lodge in Bath were 'Moderns'. There is evidence of an 'Antients' lodge forming in 1762 at the Shakespeare's Head in Westgate Street, but it was short-lived.

41

In 1784, Thomas Dunckerley, a natural son of George II and the Provincial Grand Master for Somerset, warranted the creation of a new lodge in Bath, issuing it with a new order of ceremony that he had been commissioned to produce by Premier Grand Lodge in London. Initial meetings were held in private rooms in Queens Square, but the following year the older Bear Inn Lodge amalgamated with this new Lodge and the combination was renamed The Royal Cumberland Lodge, in honour of the Duke of Cumberland and Strathearn, the then Grand Master in London. Royal Cumberland Lodge is numbered 41, showing it to be one of the oldest in continuous operation in England. It still meets regularly at Orchard Street where, in 2008, it celebrated its 275th anniversary. To this day it uses the ceremonies presented to it by Thomas Dunckerley, one of very few in the country still doing so.

In 1812, a new Antients lodge met for the first time at the Bladud's Head Inn in Walcot Street. Two years later the then Grand Master, the Duke of Sussex, conferred upon it his permission for it to be the first to be named in his honour, as Royal Sussex Lodge. Prince Augustus Frederick, Duke of Sussex, was the sixth son of George III. Upon becoming Grand Master of Premier Grand Lodge, one of his first duties was to confirm the unification of the Antients and Moderns into the United Grand Lodge of England, of which he was created the first Grand Master. He held this position over the next thirty years until his death in 1843, by which time the union was firmly cemented.

Five years after conferring his name on Royal Sussex Lodge, he visited Bath to take part in the dedication of a new purpose-built Masonic Hall in York Street. Here is part of the press report from the *'Bath Chronicle'* on Saturday 30th September 1819:

"The festival took place on Thursday when, the weather being extremely fine, the town was crowded with an assemblage of beauty and fashion that has not been equalled perhaps in the memory of the oldest inhabitant. There never was known so great an influx of strangers as thronged to witness this ceremony, conducted with that splendour which always characterises the processions of the honourable fraternity. The streets, at an early hour, assumed the appearance of the greatest bustle and expectation; at every window and house-top in the intended line of procession, groups of spectators of every degree, from the lady of title to the humblest domestic, were situated. The procession moved from the Guildhall, to the number of between 800 and 900 brethren, decorated with different orders, emblems, ensigns and ornaments, many of them of the most elegant and costly description. They proceeded up Broad Street, and when the Bath Royal

Sussex Lodge arrived opposite the York House, the procession halted, and the brethren dividing, the Royal Grand Master passed through them to join his Grand Lodge, and walked uncovered down Milsom, Union, and Stall Streets, to the Masonic Hall in York Street, returning most graciously the salutations of the immense throng, consisting of nearly the whole population of the City and surrounding country, who delighted with the interesting appearance of the sacred craft, gave way to them to pass unobstructed, and otherwise conducted themselves in the most orderly and admirable fashion. The ceremony was honoured with the presence of members of the Grand Lodges of England and Ireland, and of twenty-nine Provincial Grand Lodges, including from the counties of Somerset, Bristol, Gloucester, Devonshire, Dorset, Hants, and Warwick. The line of immense length formed by these several bodies, advanced with imposing regularity, order, and solemnity; while the music, the banners, and the various emblems of the craft, heightened the effect of this magnificent sight, and added to the grandeur and animation of the scene. On the two following days, upwards of two thousand persons (chiefly ladies) paid one shilling for admission to view the Masonic paraphernalia which were displayed in due form in the hall."

Above
York House Hotel
by William Lewis
Bath Masonic Hall Trust

43

Royal Sussex Lodge, however, were not tenants of the building, as they had declined to become involved in the project, which was conducted by Royal Cumberland and two other lodges in Bath at that time, Lodge of Virtue and Royal York Lodge of Perfect Friendship. Lodge of Virtue had originated in 1769 at the Saddlers Arms, which was on the corner of Stall Street and Westgate Street, opposite the Bear Inn and next door to the White Hart. This suggests that, although the lodges were separate organisations, their meeting places at that time were never far apart. Bearing in mind that the Bear Inn Lodge moved premises the year before, it is likely that Lodge of Virtue was formed out of the Bear Inn Lodge, in one way or another. There is no history available of the Royal York Lodge, other than its name would suggest it met at the York House Hotel, a venue used by other Lodges from time to time.

The tenancy arrangement in York Street continued until 1823, when a dispute arose with the building's financier, a local wine merchant named Charles Geary who had been Master of Royal Cumberland Lodge from 1812 to 1819. This resulted in the three lodges leaving the building and holding their meetings in separate hostelries again. Conversely, in 1826 Royal Sussex took a lease on York Street where they stayed until 1831, by which date both Lodge of Virtue and Royal Lodge of Perfect Friendship had disappeared, possibly through the forming of a new Lodge based at the York House.

Royal Cumberland set-up at the White Lion, a large coaching inn on the corner of Bridge Street and the High Street, where the northern extension of the Guildhall now stands, but did so without their Lodge equipment. This was due to what became known as 'The Bath Furniture Incident', whereby Charles Geary confiscated all Masonic furniture and possessions by locking them in the building for several years. Eventually, he offered the lot for sale at 100 guineas, the Loyal Lodge of Barnstaple in North Devon purchasing everything before the Bath Lodges were aware of the situation.

From 1843 until this day, the Masters of Royal Cumberland and the Loyal occasionally visit each other and make a special toast to the Bath Furniture. When the meeting is held in Barnstaple, the toast is *".. that it will ever remain where it now is"* and when in Bath *"..that it will soon return to its rightful owners"*.

In 1834, three Lodges took out a lease on a new hall in The Corridor, a shopping arcade that had recently opened opposite the Guildhall, where it still remains to this day. These were Royal Cumberland, Royal Sussex and a relatively new Lodge, The Lodge of Honour, which had formed in 1825, meeting at The Royal York Hotel in George Street. By the 1850s, however, they were all meeting again in local inns and hostelries, Royal Sussex at the Christopher Hotel in the High Street, just below the Corridor, Royal Cumberland at The Castle on the corner of Northgate Street and New Bond Street, and Lodge of Honour back at the Royal York Hotel.

By 1865, the members of Royal Sussex Lodge had become tired of this nomadic existence and resolved to find a permanent home. There were a number of proposals, including building another new hall, but eventually they settled on purchasing the then vacant Orchard Street Chapel from the Diocese of Clifton, together with numbers 2 and 5 Pierrepont Place, which were the old presbytery and lodging house. The total cost, including the conversion work for a Masonic Temple, came to £650.

Right
The banners of the three oldest Bath Lodges
From left to right Royal Cumberland No.41, Royal Sussex No. 53 and Lodge of Honour No. 379
Photos Paul Mallon

Bath Masonic Hall

The interior of the Temple that you see today is ostensibly how it looked when it was dedicated by Royal Sussex Lodge on 3rd December 1866, since when it has remained virtually in constant use by the organisation. Two years later, the other two Bath Lodges, Royal Cumberland and Lodge of Honour, took–up sub-tenancies.

The main changes from the chapel layout included the removal of the church pews, some of which were used to make the two wooden screens down each side of the Temple, and the erection of a wall between the pillars supporting the boxes at the rear of the auditorium, to form an ante-room out of what was the original theatre entrance foyer.

Left
The Temple at Bath Masonic Hall painting by H Gibbins
Bath Masonic Hall Trust

In 1881, to further ornament the temple, a Reredos panel was acquired. This is believed to have originally stood in St Mary's Chapel in Queen Square, one of Wood's early gems, which had been demolished to make way for a new road linking the square to the Midland Railway station at Green Park. The panels on the reredos were repainted by the local artist, John Joseph Barker.

Although it was a huge benefit to the Lodges to have a purpose-fitted building for their meetings, it was still necessary for those members that wished to attend the dinner to repair to a nearby licensed establishment. So, in 1889, proposals were put forward to create a dining room within the building. In November of that year the proposals were adopted to spend 689 pounds and 19 shillings on removing the remnants of the boxes and inserting an upper wall at the rear of the Temple. The space created behind this was used to form a dining room. An additional 289 pounds 18 shillings and nine pence were also earmarked for furnishings.

Above
View looking East showing the walls inserted to create the Ante-Room and Dining Room. The original box support columns are still visible.
Photo Dan Brown
Top Right
The Reredos
Photo Mark Gibson
Right
Royal Albert Edward No.906
Lodge Banner
Photo Paul Mallon

Because of the shared nature of the investment, a Trust Committee was set-up to oversee the works and to manage the buildings thereafter. Trustees were voted from each Craft Lodge and the same arrangement still exists today. The dining room was ready for the start of the 1890 season, when a fourth lodge, Royal Albert Edward, which had evolved as a daughter lodge of Royal Cumberland, also took up residence at Orchard Street.

Records show that the organ, as played by William Herschel in the 18th century, was purchased from the Octagon Chapel in 1896, presumably to replace the instrument left behind by the Catholic congregation. However, it was never installed in Orchard Street, a report by the Organ Committee dated 19th November 1896 advising:

**Below
Norman Bros &
Beard Organ**
Photo Paul Mallon

"In the month of April last, the organ of the Octagon Chapel was purchased in somewhat of a hurry under the impression that it would be available for use in the Masonic Hall, just as it was. Upon examination, it was found that the instrument was much too cumbersome. If placed on the dais, it would occupy the whole space between the sidewall and the pillars; if placed at the west end, it would project considerably in front of the Senior Warden's pedestal. An estimate was obtained of the cost of re-arranging the organ, so as to adapt it to the hall, which was in excess of the cost of a new organ."

The Herschel organ was subsequently sold and consideration was given to purchasing a new instrument to be designed and constructed by Griffen & Stroud, the Bath Organ Builders. However, eventually the proceeds were used to purchase a Norman Bros & Beard organ from the newly-closed Bath Spa College, previously Vellore House, which Griffen & Stroud rebuilt and installed the following year. This is the instrument you see today on the right-hand side of the stage. It was originally powered by a hydraulic water engine, but was converted to electrical power as part of the refurbishments carried-out in the 1920s. Towards the end of the century, members found it increasingly difficult to play, and its use became supplemented by a series of electronic keyboards, with the wind organ eventually falling into disuse. However, it was restored to full working order in 2009 and is now played regularly again by experienced organists within the membership.

Electrical wiring was originally installed around the turn of the century and renewed in 1923, as part of the refurbishment that took place in that year. When the building was fully-rewired in 2009, some of it was found to be still in situ!

48

PART FOUR

THE PEOPLE

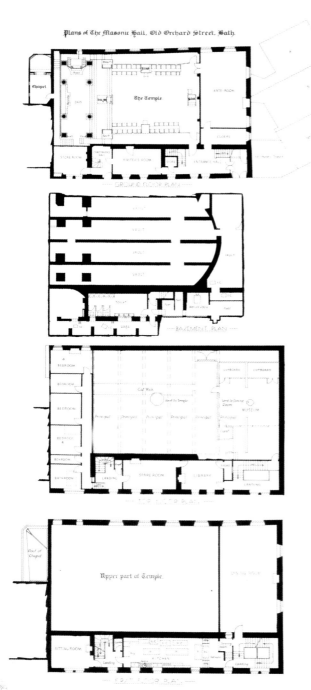

Plans of The Masonic Hall, Old Orchard Street, Bath.

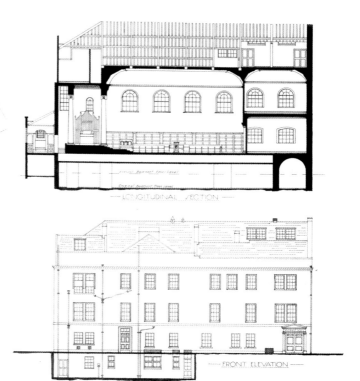

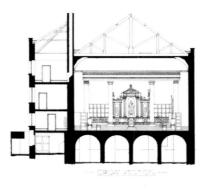

Architectural plans and elevations of the Building showing the various phases of construction. The plan of the vaults (second down on the left) reveals the original footprint of the building with a curved rear wall. The end elevation (lower right) shows the original width before the additions were made to the street frontage
Bath Masonic Hall Trust

Influential Bathonians

An historic building is not just about stone, wood and glass; those elements may provide the fabric of something that will, with care, survive the centuries of change and move through time without moving through space. Thus, by being there as a fixture, it creates a form of time-machine, not one that can actively move through dimensions, but one that passively allows time to move through it. Plans, like those shown opposite, can reveal the evolution of the layout, essentially the basic building blocks of its history, but to be truly historical it needs something more, something that only the people that use it can provide.

Life at number 12 Orchard Street has, thus far, had three distinct and separate generations, but all three have been linked by one constant: performance. In its early days, the building experienced the adulation that actors would receive from their audiences, through their interpretation of the emotions expressed by the playwrights and satirists of the day. In its next phase, it witnessed the solemnity of worship and how a congregation would be invigorated by the interpretation of scripture presented from the pulpit. Now, in its current usage, it regularly observes the esoteric ceremony derived from knowledge stretching back to the dawn of time preserved, not by a secret society as some believe it to be, but by a society that treasures its secrets.

The building has thus, survived over 250 years of, often turbulent, history. During that time many well-known Bathonians, whether born and bred or adopted, have either influenced that history, or moved regularly within its walls. Some you have already met in previous chapters. There are many others who, although they may not have left their imprint on the building as indelibly as the stonemasons, carpenters and glaziers that worked on it, they have without doubt left their mark on the City of Bath itself. In the following pages are short biographies of some of them:

Sarah Siddons
(1755 – 1831)

Opposite
Sarah Siddons
by Sir Thomas
Lawrence
Tate Gallery, London
Right
Commemorative
Plaque by the
entrance to the
Masonic Hall
Photo Paul Mallon
Below
The Shoulder of
Mutton c1900
*Photo by kind permission
of Brecknock Museum &
Art Gallery*

Sarah Siddons is considered to have been one of the greatest English tragic actresses that ever walked the boards. It was a reputation earned through a career that stretched for nearly 40 years, but that got off to a somewhat inauspicious start. In fact, it may have been a much more short-lived career, but for the four seasons spent in residence at the Bath Theatre Royal in Orchard Street between 1778 and 1782, a period that is marked by a large bronze plaque next to the entrance to the building.

Sarah was born on 5th July 1755 in a lodging room at the Shoulder of Mutton public house in Brecon, a market town in Mid-Wales. It is now renamed 'The Sarah Siddons Inn' in her honour. Her father, Roger Kemble, and her mother, also named Sarah, were members of a band of strolling players who were performing in the town, so the theatre was always a part of her life from those very early days.

Their company constantly toured the area between South Wales and the Midlands and, as a small child, Sarah was accustomed to making appearances as an extra. Nevertheless her mother, who was a Catholic, made sure that all of her children received a good education by consistently placing them in the better schools of the towns they toured though. When of age, the boys were sent away to Catholic seminaries and the eldest, John Phillip, finished his education at the Benedictine monastery at Douai.

Sarah was the eldest child in a family of twelve, four of whom, her brothers John, Charles and Stephen plus sister Elizabeth Whitlock, also became renowned stage actors, as did some of their children and grandchildren, making the Kemble family one of the more prestigious acting dynasties. Another sister, Ann Hatton, was a popular novelist of the early 19th Century. Sarah's first documented appearance in a specific role was at 11 years of age, as Ariel in Shakespeare's *"The Tempest"*, shortly after her father took over the management of the company from his wife's father John Ward.

In 1767, a young actor from Walsall named William Siddons joined the company. A few years later, he and the 16-year-old Sarah had become infatuated with each other, but their requests to be married were resisted by her parents, who preferred the suit of the son of a Herefordshire squire. In frustration, William Siddons improvised an impassioned public appeal into one evening's performance, but Sarah's father was less than impressed and dismissed Siddons from the company. To complete the separation, Sarah's mother arranged for her to be sent to a situation as a ladies maid in Warwickshire.

Whilst in service, Sarah would perform recitals in the servant's hall, the popularity of which meant that she was often asked to repeat them before visiting aristocracy. The separation from her family was reconciled in 1773, she and Siddons being given permission to marry the same year. Following their wedding, they both joined a theatre company in Cheltenham. Her tragic performances there, particularly as Belvidera in Thomas Otway's *"Venice Preserv'd"*, soon came to the attention of David Garrick, the theatrical producer and owner of the Theatre Royal in Drury Lane. A performance as Rosalind in Shakespeare's *"As You Like It"* earned her an engagement at Drury Lane in 1775, but it did not turn out successfully. She was not retained, a decision she later referred to as being *"..banished from Drury Lane as a worthless candidate for fame and fortune."*

By then she had two small children of her own, Henry and Sally, but was not inclined to take them on tour in the manner that she had lived as a child, so when the offer came along of a residency in what was then the most prestigious theatre outside of London, the Theatre Royal in Bath, she accepted it gratefully. The family initially took up residence at number 2 Abbey Green, just a few moments walk from the theatre. Sarah wrote of these early days in Bath:

"There my talents and industry were encouraged by the greatest indulgence, and, I may say, with some admiration. Tragedies again resumed their proper interest, but still I had the mortification of being obliged to personate many subordinate characters in comedy, the first being, by contract, in the possession of another lady. To this I was obliged to forfeit a part of my salary, which was only three pounds a week. After the rehearsal at Bath, and on a Monday morning, I had to go and act at Bristol on the evening of the same day; and reaching Bath again, after a drive of twelve miles, I was obliged to represent some fatiguing part there on the Tuesday evening. I wonder that I had strength and courage to support it, interrupted as I was by the cares of a mother, and by the childish sports of my little ones, who were often most unwillingly hushed to silence from interrupting their mother's studies."

**Above Right
Sarah Siddons**
by Thomas Beach
*By kind permission of
Auckland Art Gallery,
Toi o Tamaki, New
Zealand*

The cramped central location was not wholly suitable and an opportunity came to move to one of the larger, more fashionable, new town houses slightly out of the city centre. So the family took up residence at 33 The Paragon, where the building, now called Siddons House, bears a plaque commemorating this, unveiled by Ellen Terry in 1922. During their time at The Paragon, Sarah had several more pregnancies, only one of which was successful, producing her second daughter, Maria.

Whilst in Bath, she became acquainted with a former Bath resident, the father of the playwright Richard Sheridan, whose plays she appeared in regularly at Orchard Street to rapturous acclaim. She was now the darling of the Bath audiences, receiving the greatest reception for her tragic roles, in particular as Shakespeare's Lady Macbeth, a role she would make her own over the course of her career. Richard Sheridan had taken over from Garrick as the proprietor at Drury Lane London and, in 1782, he persuaded her to return there for a performance as Isabella in Thomas Southerne's *A Fatal Marriage*. These events were recorded by Sheridan's niece, Mrs Le Fanu:

"My Grandfather was strongly solicited to go to the play, to witness the performance of a young actress, who was said to distance all competition in tragedy. He found, to his astonishment, that it was the lady who had made so little impression some years before, but who was possessed of tragic powers sufficient to delight and electrify an audience. After the play was over he went behind the scenes, in order to compliment her. He said: 'I am surprised, Madame, that with such talents you should confine yourself to the country; talents that would be sure of commanding, in London, fame and success.' The actress modestly replied that she had already tried London, but without the success which had been anticipated, and that she was advised by her friends to be content with the fame and profit she obtained at Bath. Immediately on his return to London, he spoke to my uncle, strenuously recommending her to him."

Although somewhat reluctant to return after her previous experiences in London, this time her performance was a sensation and she agreed to join the Drury Lane company permanently, after completing her season in Bath. Before her farewell performance at Orchard Street, she made an emotional address to the audience, who had packed into the auditorium beyond it's capacity:

"Have I not raised some expectation here? Wrote by herself? What! authoress and player?
True, we have heard her, thus I guess'd you'd say, With decency recite another's lay;
But never heard, nor ever could we dream Herself had sipp'd the Heliconian stream.
Perhaps you farther said Excuse me pray, For thus supposing all that you might say
What will she treat of in this same address, Is it to shew her learning? - Can you guess?
Here let me answer No; far different views Possess'd my soul, and fir'd my virgin Muse;
'Twas honest gratitude, at whose request Shamed be the heart that will not do its best.
The time draws nigh when I must bid adieu To this delightful spot nay ev'n to you
To you, whose fost'ring kindness rear'd my name, O'erlooked my faults, but magnified my fame.
How shall I bear the parting? Well I know Anticipation here is daily woe.
Oh! could kind Fortune, where I next am thrown, Bestow but half the candour you have shewn.
Envy o'ercome, will hurl her pointless dart, And critic gall be shed without its smart,
The numerous doubts and fears I entertain, Be idle all as all possess'd in vain.
But to my promise. If I thus am blessed, In friendship link'd, beyond my worth caress'd,
Why don't I here, you'll say, content remain, Nor seek uncertainties for certain gain?
What can compensate for the risks you run; And what your reasons? Surely you have none.
To argue here would but your time abuse: I keep my word my reason I produce"

Below
Mrs Siddons as
Isabella
by William Hamilton
The Art Archive, Garrick Club, London
The boy in this painting is her eldest son Henry

At this cue her three children, Henry, Sally and Maria, were brought onto the stage. She had hidden them in her dressing room up to that point. She continued:

"These are the moles that bear me from your side;
Where I was rooted where I could have died.
Stand forth, ye elves, and plead your mother's cause;
Ye little magnets, whose soft influence draws
Me from a point where every gentle breeze, Wafted my bark to happiness and ease
Sends me adventurous on a larger main, In hopes that you may profit by my gain.
Have I been hasty? am I then to blame; Answer, all ye who own a parent's name?
Thus have I tried you with an untaught Muse,
Who for your favour still most humbly sues,
That you, for classic learning, will receive
My soul's best wishes, which I freely give
For polished periods round, and touched with art,
The fervent offering of my grateful heart."

In her first season at Drury Lane, London audiences flocked to see her repeat her previous successes with the roles that she had become famous for in Bath such as Belvidera, Rosalind and Lady Macbeth. One contemporary review read: *"Men wept, and women fainted, or were carried out in fits of hysterics."* She was acknowledged in the press as *"The finest tragic actress now on the English stage."*

The following year, she was appointed by King George III and Queen Charlotte as Reader in English to the Royal Children, despite the royal couple's well-documented antipathy towards the theatre. With crowds lining the street outside of the theatre simply to catch a glimpse, her stardom was confirmed. She would stay at Drury Lane for the next twenty years, expanding her repertoire to include other Shakespearian roles such as Desdemona and Ophelia. But two of the tragic roles that she was particularly successful in were thanks to Shakespearian revivals produced by her brother John Philip Kemble. These were as Volumnia in *"Coriolanus"* and, most memorably, as Queen Katherine in *"Henry VIII"*, a role that some observed was as perfect for her as Lady Macbeth.

Left
Sarah Siddons
by Gilbert Stuart
Below
Malpomene
by James Gillray
Both National Portrait Gallery, London
Cartoonists like Gillray were the tabloid press of their day, and no famous person was spared their sharp wit. This cartoon refers to the perception at the time that money was Mrs Siddons' prime motivation.

All of this success in the capital, however, did not mean that she was entirely lost to her Bath admirers and, despite her hectic schedule, she occasionally made special appearances on stage at Orchard Street for benefit performances, guaranteeing the promoters a complete sell-out at premium prices.

Nevertheless, her meteoric rise to stardom, coupled with a number of miscarriages, began to cause her to suffer from exhaustion and ill-health. This occasionally meant that she missed performances, which began to be interpreted as selfishness by the press, most notably when she was unable to appear in a benefit in Dublin. The

resultant negative publicity caused her to be jeered and catcalled at her next opening night in London, the constant uproar that night eventually causing her to faint on the stage. Once she had recovered her composure, she addressed the audience in an attempt to both explain and apologise. The stress of it all caused her to even contemplate giving-up acting altogether and, coupled with financial difficulties, this all began to put a strain on her marriage to William Siddons, which eventually resulted in an informal separation, but not divorce.

It was during one of her visits back to Orchard Street that she became re-acquainted with a young painter, Thomas Lawrence, who she had met originally whilst resident at the theatre. When Lawrence arrived in London, he became romantically involved with both of Sarah's daughters in turn, which ended tragically for all involved when the younger daughter, Maria, died. After the subsequent death of her other daughter Sally, Sarah maintained an intimate friendship with the painter, who produced several paintings of her, the most stunning of which is his portrait from 1797, shown at the beginning of this chapter, thought to be depicting her as the adulterous Mrs Haller in *"The Stranger"*.

People often believe that mass hysteria surrounding the visit of a popular artist is quite a modern phenomenon. But when Sarah Siddons returned to Orchard Street in February 1799 to perform in a benefit for William Dimond, the popular proprietor who was shortly to retire from acting and would be playing a lead role for the final time, the approaches to the theatre were crowded, even during rehearsals, with people anxious to see this famous star. Similar scenes were repeated wherever she went in the City throughout her stay. Bearing in mind that there were no means of electronic communication back then, and despite it only being announced in the Theatre late on the Saturday evening that she would be appearing the following week, the Bath Herald newspaper reported that *"at an early hour on Monday there was not a seat unlet for any of her performances."*

63

The chosen play for the benefit was *"The Grecian Daughter"* where Sarah was cast in one of her signature roles, that of Euphrasia. In unprecedented scenes before the play began, theatregoers fought for places and more money was taken at the door than had ever been before. Many who had purchased tickets in advance could not get in and the resultant uproar meant that the first scenes of the play could not be heard. It was hoped that when Mrs Siddons appeared that the situation would calm down, but instead the applause was so great that it was impossible for the actors to continue. Eventually they all left the stage and the constable was summoned. After a while order was returned, allowing the performance to start again from the beginning.

In 1803, she and her brother left Drury Lane and moved to the rival company two streets away at Covent Garden. It was there on June 29th 1812 that she made her farewell performance, inevitably as Lady Macbeth. By all accounts, that night the audience would not allow the play to proceed beyond the sleepwalking scene, the part of the role where her unique interpretation, stopping to lay down the candle to concentrate on washing her hands, always held the audience spellbound.

Above
Sarah Siddons and
John Phillip
Kemble in
"Macbeth "
by Thomas Beach
Left
Sarah Siddons as
Lady Macbeth
by George Henry Harlow
Both from The Art Archive, Garrick Club, London

For a few years after her official retirement, she continued to make occasional benefit appearances, mainly for members of her wider family. It would seem from contemporary reports that these later performances were ill-advised, one somewhat spiteful reviewer observing that:

"The loss of teeth rendered her articulation very indistinct, and she occasionally whistled, which, as the character was not a musical one, was by no means effective."

She died at her home in London aged 76 on May 31st 1831. She is buried in St Mary's Churchyard, Paddington. A statue was erected to her in Westminster Abbey, near to one of her brother John Philip Kemble, who had died in 1823. Proof that tragedy in her life was not confined to her stage performances is borne-out by the fact that she not only survived her younger brother, but also her husband, all but two of her children and Sir Thomas Lawrence.

Over the next sixty years her memory faded from public life. When her great grandson, Henry George Impey Siddons, visited her grave in the late 19th century during a visit from India where he worked as a schoolteacher, he found it in an appalling state. He restored it and was also instrumental in having the statue erected nearby, prior to his subsequent retirement to Bath. On his death there in 1936, at the age of 84, he was the last surviving direct descendant of Sarah Siddons. As he had no heirs, he left a watch owned by his grandfather, Sarah's younger son George, to the then Duke of Kent. This has since passed to the present Duke of Kent, who is the current Grand Master of the United Grand Lodge of England. The bequest read as follows:

Above
Statue of Sarah
Siddons erected in
Paddington Green by
her great grandson
Photo Simon White

"I trust that, as I have no heir to leave it to, his Royal Highness Prince George, Duke of Kent, will be graciously pleased to accept the gold repeater watch given by His Majesty King George IV, to his Godson, my grandfather, George Siddons, of the Bengal Civil Service. From Royalty it came, to Royalty it should return."

From the many portraits of her exhibited in galleries around the world, it is obvious that, as well as being a great actress, she was also a very beautiful woman. She was once described as *"tall with a striking figure, extraordinary beauty, powerfully expressive eyes, and a solemn dignity of demeanour that enables her to confer a weird majesty on the character, inexpressibly heightening the tragic awe surrounding her fate."*

Gainsborough's portrait, painted shortly after her return to the London stage, shows this well, but the one painting that most closely resembles that description is by Sir Joshua Reynolds and is entitled *"Sarah Siddons as the Tragic Muse"*. It was first exhibited at the Royal Academy in 1784 and became an iconic image of its time.

It is so powerful an image that over 150 years later, in 1952, it proved to be the inspiration for a Hollywood movie entitled *"All About Eve"* starring Bette Davis. So successful was this film, that it was nominated for every category in that year's Oscars ceremony, a feat only equalled to this day by one other movie, *'Titanic'* in 1997. Curiously, the movie featured a storyline that revolved around an awards ceremony organised by the Sarah Siddons Society, where a young actress was presented with the Sarah Siddons Award. The movie begins with the camera panning-out from the Joshua Reynolds portrait, which is hanging in pride of place in the Society's banqueting room.

Left
Sarah Siddons
by Thomas Gainsborough
The National Gallery, London

Far Right
Sarah Siddons as the Tragic Muse
by Sir Joshua Reynolds
The Huntington Library, Art Collections & Botanical Gardens, San Marino, California

At the time, both the award and the society were purely fictional inventions of the writers of the screenplay, but in one of those ironic twists of history, the incredible success of the movie inspired a group of Hollywood actors to create, in 1954, their own version of the Sarah Siddons Society, which every two years since has presented a real Sarah Siddons Award to an actor that has produced an outstanding stage performance.

Some may say this is merely fact mimicking fiction, but maybe it is the incredible charismatic personality of probably the most revered stage actress of all time, conveyed through time by the work of possibly the most gifted portrait painter of his age, to weave it's extraordinary magic once again.

Bishop Peter Augustine Baines
(1786 – 1843)

Peter Augustine Baines was born into a farming family in Lancashire and was initially educated in an English Benedictine Monastery in Lamspringe, near Hanover. When the monastery was suppressed by the Prussian Government in 1802, he returned with the monks to Ampleforth in Yorkshire, where he completed his education and was ordained in 1810. Baines never lacked in self-confidence, probably due to his sharp intellect, but when this was combined with the distinct lack of humility he exhibited towards his more conservative elders, it produced the type of controversy that would follow him throughout what would be, in everything other than political strategy, a brilliant career. These tendencies emerged early in his career when, as a novice, he was instrumental in having the founding Prior of Ampleforth, Father Appleton, replaced by Dr Brewer, the President General of the Benedictine Mission, and the same Dr Brewer who had fled for his life through the streets of Bath years earlier.

Regardless of this ability to inadvertently ruffle even the calmest of feathers, often interpreted as arrogance, he was extremely popular among his friends and the parishioners that he ministered to. He worked tirelessly at his pastoral work, administering to the sick and dying without a thought to his own comforts, even sleeping on the floors of houses rather than leave a parishioner who he felt was in need of his attendance.

Above Right
Lamspringe Abbey
as it is today
Photo by kind permission of Lamspringe Town Council

Left
Bishop Baines by
an unknown artist
Reproduced by kind permission of Prior Park School, Bath
Photo Paul Mallon

69

He was a popular preacher and it was said of him at the time that "*a church which was nearly empty when preachers of inferior mark occupied it, was crowded when Father Baines was announced as the orator.*" His abilities in this area were almost theatrical and, like a previous occupant of the stage at Orchard Street, his dramatic delivery could move the audience to tears. He preached regularly at the Orchard Street Chapel, attracting crowds from congregations beyond his own, as illustrated by these remarks from John Skinner, the Anglican Vicar of Camerton, in his '*Journal of a Somerset Rector*':

"*Having understood that the new Catholic Bishop, Mr Baines, was to preach on Corpus Christi, I accompanied Mr Haggard and my brother Russell to the Chapel in Bath after breakfast. I shall not attempt a description of the ceremonies employed, sufficient is it to say that no acting during the time the Chapel was a theatre could exceed what we then witnessed. With regard to the subject of Mr Baines' discourse, delivered, I must do him the credit to say, in a very impressive manner, the delusive turn respecting corporeal and spiritual by no means benefitted his argument with men of reading or reflection. I am speaking of the Protestant part of his hearers, who appeared to be very numerous, considering the admission to the Chapel was two shillings apiece for those of a different community.*"

The other aspect of his character that often brought him into conflict scenarios, was the combination of expensive tastes coupled with an apparent inability to understand basic financial principles. He was not of noble birth, so he had no private income, but if ever there was a person who could have benefitted from having Wilkins Micawber's later maxim regarding income and expenditure embroidered on his cassock, it was Peter Baines. Even within his first weeks away from the stability of Ampleforth, he had to approach his Benedictine sponsors in Bath for additional funding after spending more than his entire stipend on furnishings for his new presbytery in Pierrepont Place.

However, this was never to stop him from realising a vision, mainly thanks to an extension to his theatrical abilities that enabled him to persuade even the most doubting listener that a scheme was worthy of support, particularly financial support. He was gregarious with an easy manner, allowing him to mix with all classes of parishioner, particularly the female nobility, of which there were many that attended Orchard Street, although there was never any hint of impropriety, as he was completely dedicated to his calling.

In 1823, he was made co-adjutor to Bishop Collingridge, which also brought him the title of Bishop of Siga. His no-frills approach to his new duties began to earn him enemies, including an ex-prefect at Lamspringe, Reverend Birdsall, who was appointed to Benedictine Provincial in the same year. Birdsall would prove somewhat of a nemesis for Baines during most of the rest of his career.

Baines' dream was to establish a Catholic university in England and his first moves towards that were to attempt to establish a seminary at Downside, but this was not a popular idea with the Benedictine community there. So as soon as he succeeded to the Vicar Apostolic post in 1829, he took his proposals to Rome, where they received approval, but only by making even greater waves among the Benedictines at Downside and at his old seminary at Ampleforth.

On his return he purchased Prior Park mansion, the former home of Ralph Allen, but did so without holding close to sufficient funds for his purpose. It was his loyal friend from Ampleforth, Dr Brindle, that completed the transaction while Baines was away from Bath, agreeing a price of £22,000, of which Brindle paid £100 deposit and signed a mortgage for another £5,000 on Baines' behalf. The last sentence of his message to Baines confirming the purchase also reveals the situation:

"All are surprised where your Lordship has got the money. The price is not known positively — some say extravagant things."

The truth was there was no cash beyond that which Brindle had handed over, but this didn't stop Baines immediately embarking on plans for extensive building works, including the addition of two college wings, one at each end of the property, individually dedicated to St Peter and St Paul. Needless to say, it wasn't long before his wide circle of well-heeled benefactors began to advance gifts and loans, one lady alone providing most of her personal fortune of £20,000 to the project.

Bishop Baines moved into Prior Park during the following year and, over the next ten years, the college grew in both size and educational stature, although there were often financial question marks. Such controversies were always exacerbated by Baines' irascible nature, but regardless the enterprise, like his Vicariate, blossomed.

In 1840 he fell-foul of the authorities in Rome over comments he had made in his Lent Pastoral. He was summoned to Rome and kept there for nearly a year, while the matter was chewed over and a compromise reached that both parties could agree upon. Unfortunately, on his return, Baines' published version of the agreement was substantially different from Rome's interpretation and he received a severe censure from the Pope. Although outwardly, he appeared to shrug this off in his usual manner, in the aftermath he lost some standing with both loyal colleagues from the College and wealthy patrons.

It was probably the combined stress of all of this and the gathering financial clouds, that he suffered a stroke that brought about his untimely and sudden death at Prior Park in 1843. At the two-day lying in state, upwards of thirteen thousand people of all denominations travelled to Prior Park, some from hundreds of miles away, to pass round the catafalque. However, the funeral itself was not attended by any high officials of the church, a contrast that clearly illustrates the differing emotions the man could engender in those that met him. Yet all would agree on one point - that it was difficult to ignore him.

After his death, Prior Park College inevitably fell foul of internal church politics and was sold. It was repurchased in 1866 by Bishop Clifford, and remains an independent Catholic school to this day. When the Bishop's staff were making their inspection after the repurchase, they were amazed to find Baines' coffin in a store room. It had been placed there awaiting interment in the new chapel that was being constructed when he died, but as the work had never been completed, neither had the burial.

The coffin was removed and buried in the cemetery at Downside, where it remained until 1909, when the authorities there decided that he merited higher recognition and re-interred him within the Abbey Church. At the ceremony, Abbot Kindersley uttered probably the best epitaph for the man:

"I have at last managed to bring the Bishop of Siga into our church, and I hope that, having done, he will rest in peace, and bring us peace as well."

**Right
Bishop Baines'
Tomb** in
Downside Abbey
*Photo courtesy of
Downside Abbey Trustees*

ROBERT DYER COMMANS
1862   CHARLES F. MARSHALL
1863   EDWARD TURNER PAYNE
1864   WILLIAM F. BENNETT
1865   JOHN LUM STOTHERT
1866   CHARLES R. DAVY REV.
1867   WILLIAM GIBBS
1868   JOSEPH HOL

John Lum Stothert
(1829 – 1891)

John Lum Stothert was the Master of Royal Sussex Lodge in 1865 when it purchased the former Catholic Chapel in Old Orchard Street. He was the grandson of George Stothert, who founded the original ironmongery business in Horse Street, Bath (now Southgate Street) in the mid 1780s. From those small beginnings, subsequent generations of the family built-up the various engineering companies that evolved, culminating in what would be one of the largest employers in Bath for well over 100 years, Stothert & Pitt.

In the early part of the 19th Century, the Stothert family manufactured and sold a diverse range of engineering products, including Wood Planes, Pumps, Ploughs, Gas Apparatus and Bridges, often in partnership with other specialist engineers. Most of their own product lines were originally developed from their foundry premises established in 1815 by George Stothert Junior in Newark Street, behind his father's shop in Horse Street. The foundry was taken over in 1827 by Henry Stothert, George Senior's younger son by his second marriage, due to George Junior's early retirement abroad because of ill-health. It would be Henry that would take the family business to new levels thanks to the rapid advances in engineering brought about by the industrial revolution.

Henry's son, John Lum Stothert, was educated as an engineer and apprenticed during the late 1840s at the Avonside Iron Works in Bristol, founded in 1837 by his father. Subsequently, first as Stothert & Slaughter then as the Avonside Engine Co. Ltd, they became heavily involved with the manufacture of railway locomotives throughout the rest of the 19th Century. They produced broad gauge mainline locomotives for the major railway companies, including Brunel's Great Western, as well as smaller Tank Locomotives that were used for branch lines and shunting, such as on docksides. One of these tank locomotives is still in use, transporting visitors to the restored SS Great Britain along the preserved Quayside Railway in Bristol.

Stothert & Slaughter also owned a Shipyard in Bristol Docks from which they supplied a wide range of iron-hulled vessels, including at least two supply ships, each of over 1,000 tons, used for the Crimean War effort in the early 1850s. So it is not difficult to see how the evolution occurred into the design and construction of what would become the Company's main product line for over 150 years, dockyard cranes.

By the early 1850s Henry Stothert had retired and John moved to Bath to head-up the cranes operation in partnership with Robert Pitt. The latter had joined the Company as an apprentice in 1834, ten years later becoming a partner in the foundry business, which was renamed Stothert, Rayno & Pitt in 1844. Robert Pitt was also a member of Royal Sussex Lodge, having been initiated on the same date as John Lum Stothert, so the two men were clearly close friends as well as business partners.

Below
Robert Pitt
By Kind Permission of the Pitt Family
Below left
Newark Works c1870 by an unknown artist
Bath in Time / Bath Central Library Collection

The company rapidly outgrew the existing foundry and, in 1857, Stothert & Pitt moved to a new enlarged factory at Newark Works across the river on the Lower Bristol Road. John Lum Stothert remained at Newark Works until his retirement from the day-to-day control of the company in 1883, when the partnership was incorporated into a new Limited Company. He continued as Chairman of the Limited Company until his death in 1891, after which the Company was run by Robert Pitt's son Walter.

John Lum Stothert was largely responsible for the Company's growth to later become an employer of over 2,000 people in Bath alone. He oversaw the evolution of the early steam cranes, including the development of the Fairbairn Crane design that incorporated a curved, tubular girder jib in place of the traditional straight wooden or iron one. This allowed much heavier weights to be lifted by the more compact design and one of these cranes is preserved at Princes Wharf in Bristol. From these evolved the giant block-setting crane ranges, titled Mammoth, Goliath and Titan, that were used to set in place the massive concrete blocks used in the construction of harbours and sea defences around the world, blocks that were cast locally thanks to the new range of concrete mixers also designed and manufactured at Newark Works.

His interests were not limited to the various engineering companies under his control. After retirement, he developed his interest in Astronomy, writing a number of papers for the Royal Society. He was secretary to the British Association for the Advancement of Science when it met at the Bath Institute in 1888, the very building on North Parade that was originally Simpson's Assembly Rooms.

Right
Stothert & Pitt
Titan Crane
Photo by kind permission of Bath Industrial Heritage Trust Ltd

Above
The Four Bath Worthies by an unknown artist *Bath in Time / Bath Preservation Trust*
This painting from 1735 contains possibly the only surviving image of John Wood the Elder (standing right).   The other
figures are, left to right, Richard Jones (Clerk of Works at Combe Down Stone Quarries), Richard 'Beau' Nash and
Ralph Allen .

There are two very interesting aspects of this painting. Firstly, the subject matter, which shows Jesus performing one of his miracles, as related in the Gospel of St John. Here he heals a paralysed man waiting to be admitted to the Pool at Bethesda. The Aramaic translation of Beth-esda is 'House of Mercy', and it was a renowned site in biblical times, where the infirm pilgrimaged to take the healing waters. The correlation with the City of Bath cannot be missed, especially when the artist was both patron and trustee of the most important hospital there.

However, there is a more esoteric analogy, in that Bethesda was described in the Gospels as a large pool complex with five porches, or gates, near to a sheep market. When Hoare arrived in Bath, the City was still mainly contained within its medieval walls. Unusually, these had five gates, one each at the compass points, plus the small Ham Gate that had provided the Abbey monks with a private passageway from their Abbey gardens out to the Ham, where their sheep would have been grazing. It also incorporated the drain that conveyed the waste water from the King's Bath out to the River Avon, in the process flushing the public privy located nearby. The location of the Ham Gate was at the end of what is now Old Orchard Street, and part of what is believed to be the original hot bath drain, uncovered when the vaults were excavated in 2002, can be seen in the corner of the Museum Vaults.

Above
The Pool at
Bethesda by
William Hoare
Bath Masonic Hall Trust

Cecile Agathe Adelaide Riquet de Caraman
Marquise de Sommery
(1768 - 1847)

Cecile de Sommery, as she was called during her life in Bath, was born the daughter of a French nobleman Victor Maurice de Riquet, 1st Count of Caraman, a descendent of Pierre-Paul Riquet builder of the Canal du Midi. Her mother, Marianne Chimay d'Alsace, was a Belgian princess.

Her father was a favourite of King Louis XV's father-in-law, the Duke of Lorraine, and was made Lieutenant General of the King's Armies. Louis XVI made him Governor of Provence, in which capacity during the 1789 revolution he was involved in the clandestine negotiations with the region's nobles in Marseilles surrounding his cousin, the Comte de Mirabeaux's attempts at establishing a constitutional monarchy.

This high status meant that childhood life for Cecile and her eight siblings was very comfortable, living at her father's Chateau at Roissy-en-France, north of Paris where

Charles de Gaulle airport stands today. The Chateau was surrounded by lavish English-style gardens, Victor's main interest outside of the military. This passion for garden design led to Marie Antoinette appointing him to redesign the gardens of Les Petit Trianon at Versailles in a similar fashion.

Cecile married the dashing cavalry officer Armand du Mesnil, Marquis de Sommery, in Paris in 1786, but within three years she, her husband and their baby daughter Stephanie were forced to flee their homeland as the revolution began its bloody round-up of the nobility and royalist supporters.

Left
Victor de Riquet Comte de Caraman by Alexander Roslin
Archives Charmet / The Bridgeman Art Library

Along with other French émigrés they came to Bath, where its relaxed attitude to such visitors assured them of a safe haven. As Catholics, they became part of the community that worshipped at the Corn Street Chapel.   By the time that community moved to the Orchard Street Chapel, three more children had been added to the family, Auguste, Henrietta and Pulcherie.

Armand joined the English Army as a Captain of Horse in 1791. Although this sounds unusual, it was not at that time because the French Royalist cause was supported by all of France's enemies across Europe. What started as small irregular units grew as more of their countrymen arrived in England, so that by the time the Duke of Wellington undertook the Peninsular Campaign at the start of the 19th century, there were enough émigrés in the British Army for an entire regiment to be formed, called the Chasseurs Britanniques.

The turmoil in her home country was not just dividing communities, it was dividing families as well. Cecile's father maintained his high position in the French Army until the King was executed, forcing him to emigrate in 1793. Her eldest brother Louis, who had been a leading diplomat, found himself exiled to Prussia. Victor's second son, Maurice, had moved to Austria with his family, and joined the Rohan Hussars, a regiment within the Austrian Army also formed from French émigrés similarly the Chasseurs Britanniques. The youngest son Philippe took the rest of the family across the Belgian border to his mother's home in Chimay.

Above
The Vicomtresse de Vaudreuil by Elisabeth Louise Vigee le Brun *The J Paul Getty Museum, Los Angeles*. The Vicomtesse was Victoire Pauline Riquet de Caraman, Cecile's elder sister

Then in 1811, tragedy struck when her husband, Armand, died suddenly.   Cecile decided to stay and bring-up her family in Bath. Whether this was because they were unable to return due to the political situation in France, or they had simply become settled in the City and were therefore part of the social scene, we do not know. Auguste, who had inherited his father's title aged just 18, died in London, but is buried in Bath along with his mother and sisters.

They all lived at 37 Green Park, a John Palmer-designed terrace to the west of Kingsmead, just a few doors away from where Jane Austen produced her early short works whilst living with her father after he retired to the City. That Cecile was on the social circuit is clear from this excerpt from the 1817 diary of Madame d'Arblay, the wife of another French émigré living in Bath, but better known as the novelist, Fanny Burney:

**Below
The Marquise de Sommery's
Memorial Stone**
in the Museum
Photo Andy Clist

"Alex preceded me to Madame de Sommery, who had two joilies daughters, Stephanie and Pulcherie, at work by her side, the tea table spread 'a la anglaise' and four of your theatres upon the table, with Alex just beginning 'Dido' as I entered. Madame de Sommery is much pleased with the garden possession, and full of amity and courtesy and agremous"

From what we know, Cecile was able to conduct the rest of her life in Bath with little of the stress and drama that had occurred previously. She continued to worship regularly at the Orchard Street Chapel and this is borne-out by her prayerbook, which has survived and is now in the Pitts Library at Emory University in Atlanta, Georgia. In the back of the prayerbook is a short hand-written history of her husband's life, showing that she kept his memory forever close to her heart. The kindness of that heart is commemorated by her children on her memorial stone:

"Compelled by the French Revolution to abandon a distinguished social position and to quit her native Country, she took refuge in this hospitable land. Her religious submission to the Divine Will enabled her to support with pious resignation the vicissitudes and trials of a long exile. Her life was dedicated to the affectionate duties of a wife and a mother, and to the relief and consolation of the destitute and afflicted. A model of piety, charity and virtue, she lived for the happiness of others"

John Joseph Barker
(1824 – 1904)

John Joseph Barker was a third generation member of the dynasty of painters known as the Barkers of Bath. His grandfather, Benjamin Barker, developed a keen interest in horses as a boy living on the estate of his wealthy father. When that passion extended to horse racing, he lost a considerable amount of money gambling, and was disowned by his father. He decided to become an artist and moved to Pontypool in South Wales, where he worked for Thomas Allgood decorating Japanned Ware. In 1781 he moved to Bath to work as a portrait painter, but found that he could not make sufficient money and supplemented his earnings by working for a local coachbuilder, Charles Spackman, painting coats of arms on carriages.

His eldest son, Thomas Barker, was 14 when the family moved to Bath. The boy's talent was noted by Spackman, who arranged to provide training for the young artist in return for an interest in his output. In 1790, Spackman arranged for Thomas Barker to go to Rome where he became friends with the sculptor Flaxman and set up a Society of English Art Students. Barker then lived in London for a while before returning to Bath in 1800. He commissioned the architect Gandy to build him a large house in Sion Hill with a 30-foot picture gallery to exhibit his works. This was named Doric House, after the large columns that adorned the outside. In the picture gallery, he painted a fresco entitled *The Massacre of the Sciotes* that covers one entire wall.

Right
Thomas Barker
Self Portrait
Holburne Museum of Art, Bath

Thomas Barker had four sons all of whom became artists in their own right, but at differing levels of success. The eldest, Thomas Jones Barker, trained in Paris. He specialised in Historical Military scenes and is probably the best known of that generation. The second son, Benjamin, and youngest son Octavius, were both copyists. It was later discovered that, after their father's death, the latter had forged some works attributed to his father.

John Joseph Barker was best known as a landscape artist, but in 1882 produced the three panels for the Reredos, after it was installed in the Temple at Bath Masonic Hall.

Far Left
Hiram Abiff
Centre
King Solomon
Right
Hiram King of
Tyre
The three panels in the Reredos, all by John Joseph Barker
Bath Masonic Hall Trust

Thomas Beach
(1738 – 1806)

Thomas Beach was born in Milton Abbas in Dorset. During his education at the grammar school in the town, his artistic prowess was noted by Lord Milton, who sent him to London in 1760 to study under Sir Joshua Reynolds at the Academy in St Martin's Lane. Five years later he settled in Bath to begin a career painting portraits of the fashionable visitors and residents of the city. In 1770, he moved into what would be his permanent studio for over 30 years, at number 2 Westgate Buildings, a location perfectly placed on the main carriage route from the residences on the Lansdown slopes to the Baths.

He was particularly fond of the theatre, and visited Orchard Street whenever work allowed. His diary of 1798 includes over a dozen detailed accounts of plays that he saw during the season, as well as many more entries simply recording his attendance. It was through this love of the stage that he made the acquaintance of Sarah Siddons, of whom he painted several portraits, probably the finest of which is his 1778 portrait of her reading for a part, and featured in the chapter on Mrs Siddons earlier in this book, along with his portrait of her father Roger Kemble and his stunning portrail of Sarah and her brother John Phillip Kemble in Macbeth. He was also a very close friend of John Henderson.

Right
Thomas Beach
Self Portrait from 1802
National Portrait Gallery, London

In 1786, he produced a portrait of Thomas Dunckerley. This was presented to Royal Cumberland Lodge to honour their close association with Dunckerley, who was Provincial Grand Master of Somerset at the time.

Thomas Beach himself was not a Freemason at the time of its presentation, but the Lodge minutes record that, three years later in 1789, he was initiated into the Royal Cumberland Lodge. Although he never held high office in the Lodge, his attendance was listed regularly.

The Dunckerley portrait hung in pride of place in the Royal Cumberland Lodge rooms until, in 1819, it was transferred to the new York Street Freemasons Hall along with the rest of the Lodge's furniture. This meant, of course, that it was later lost to the Lodge when all of the furniture and chattels were purchased by the Loyal Lodge at Barnstaple, in whose dining room it still hangs today.

In 1802, Beach retired to Dorchester, where he died in 1806. His self-portrait of 1802, shown overleaf, is believed to be the last of more than 300 portraits attributed to him, and now displayed in galleries throughout the world.

Left
Thomas
Dunckerley
by Thomas Beach
By kind permission of Loyal Lodge No 251, Barnstaple
Photo Paul Mallon

90

Bibliography

Andrews, Ken   *Stothert & Pitt: Cranemakers of the world* (Tempus 2003)

Ashley, Thomas P   *An Abridged History of the Royal Cumberland Lodge, No.41* (Bath 1873)

Asleson, Robyn   *A Passion for Performance, Sarah Siddons & Her Portraitists* (Getty 1999)

Barrett, Charlotte   *Diary and letters of Madame d'Arblay* (London 1846)

Bladon, S   *The Life of Mr James Quin — Comedian* (London 1766)

Borsay, Peter   *The Image of Georgian Bath, 1700-2000* (Oxford 2000)

Bryant, Heather   *Theatre Royal, Bath: a calendar of performances at the Orchard Street theatre, 1750-1805* (Bath 1977)

Buchanan, Brenda J   *Bath History Vol.6* (Bath 1996)
                      Bath History Vol.8 (Bath 2000)

Calvert, Keith W   *A short history of the Masonic Hall, Old Orchard Street* (Bath 1950)

Campbell, Thomas   *The Life of Mrs Siddons* (Bath 1840)

Clear, Charles R   *John Palmer, Mail Coach Pioneer* (Blandford 1955)

Colvin, Howard   *A Biographical Dictionary of British Architects, 1600 to 1840* (Yale 2008)

Coombs, H & C   *Journal of a Somerset Rector, 1803 to 1834* (Oxford 1984)

Cresswell, Paul   *Bath in Quotes* (Bath 2006)

Cross, Michael   *Kegs & Ale, Bath & the Public House* (Bath 1991)

Davis, Graham   *Bath exposed!: essays on the social history of Bath, 1775-1945* (Bath 2007)

Donohue, Joseph   *Cambridge History of British Theatre: 1660 to 1895* (Cambridge 2004)

Genest, John   *Some Account of the English Stage: From 1660 to 1830* (Bath 1832)

Green, Mowbray A   *The Eighteenth Century Architecture of Bath* (Bath 1904)

Gilbert, Pamela J   *This Restless Prelate: Bishop Peter Baines* (Leominster 1996)

Harper, Charles G   *The Bath Road: history, fashion, & frivolity on an old highway* (London 1899)

Hunter, Rev. Joseph   *The Connection of Bath with the Literature and Science of England* (Bath 1863)

Kenning, George   *Masonic Encyclopedia and Handbook of Masonic Archeology, History and Biography* (Kessinger Reprint 2003)

Lowndes, William   *The Theatre Royal at Bath* (Bristol 1982)

Mackintosh, Sir James   *Vindiciae Gallicae and Other Writings on the French Revolution* (Indianapolis 2006)

McDonald, Russ   *Look to the Lady: Sarah Siddons, Ellen Terry, and Judi Dench on the Shakespearean stage* (Georgia 2005)

Melville, Lewis   *Bath Under Beau Nash* (London 1907)

Murch, Jerom   *Biographical Sketches of Bath Personalities* (Bath 1843)

Neale, R. S   *Bath, A Social History 1680-1850* (London 1981)

Oliver, Rev. George   *Revelations of a Square* (London 1855)

Parsons, Mrs   *The Incomparable Siddons* (London 1909)

Peach, R.E.M   *Historic Houses in Bath and their Associations* (London 1883)
    Street Lore of Bath (London 1893)

Penley, Belville S   *The Bath Stage: A History of Dramatic Representations in Bath,* (London 1892)

Ruvigny, M   *The Nobilities of Europe* (London 1909)

Sitwell, Edith   *Bath* (London 1932)

Swift, A & Elliott, K   *The Lost Pubs of Bath* (Akeman Press 2005)

Torrens, H. S   *The Evolution of a Family Firm: Stothert and Pitt of Bath* (Bath 1978)

Trussler, Simon   *Cambridge Illustrated History of British Theatre* (Cambridge 1994)

Tyte, William   *Bath in the Eighteenth Century* (Bath 1903)

Walker, R G   *Freemasonry in the Province of Somerset 1725 - 1987* (Wells 1987)

Warner, Rev. Richard   *Excursions from Bath* (Bath 1801)

Williams, J Anthony   *Bath and Rome: The Living Link* (Bath 1963)